Cc

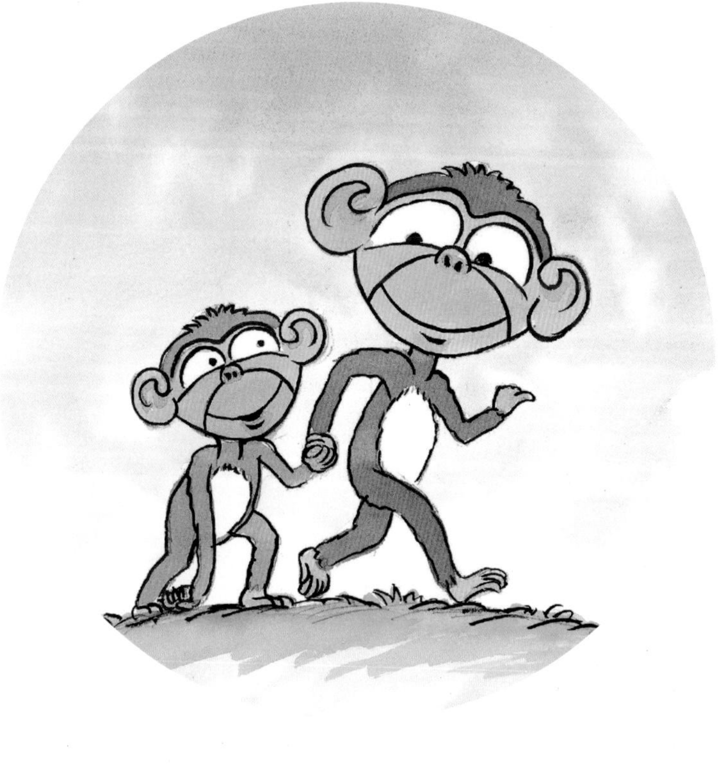

Illustrated by Dave Gunson

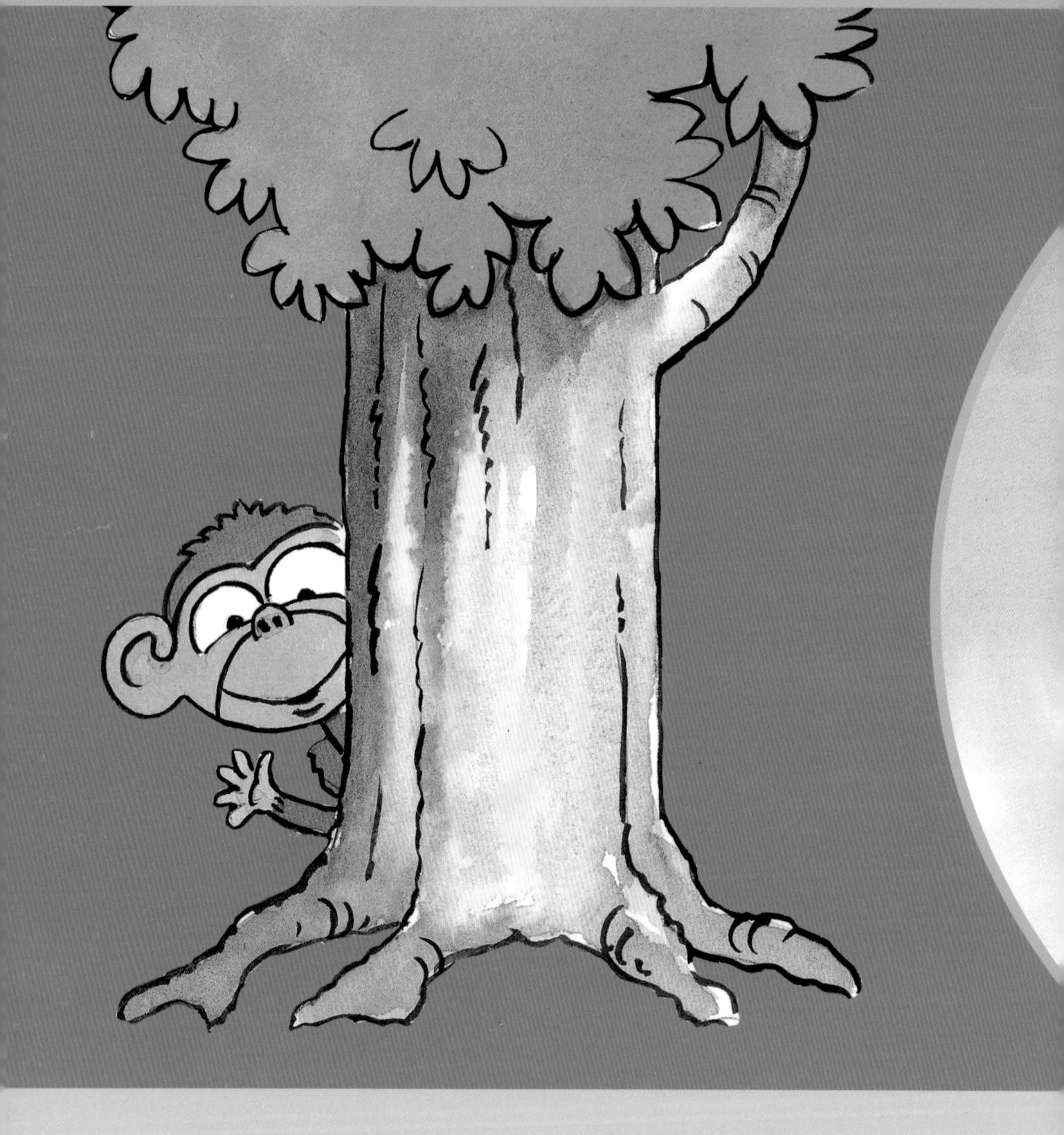

Come to the tree.

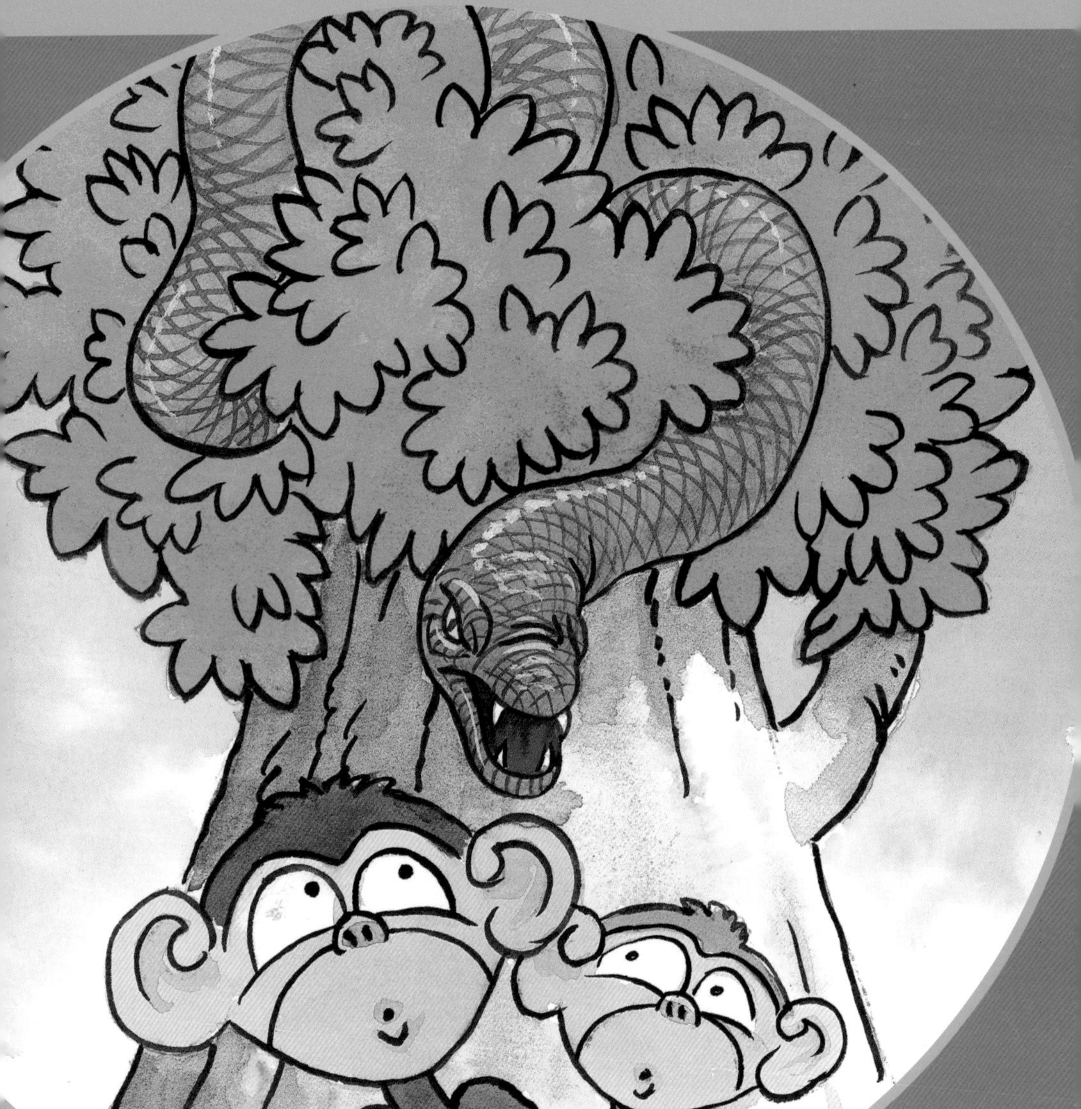

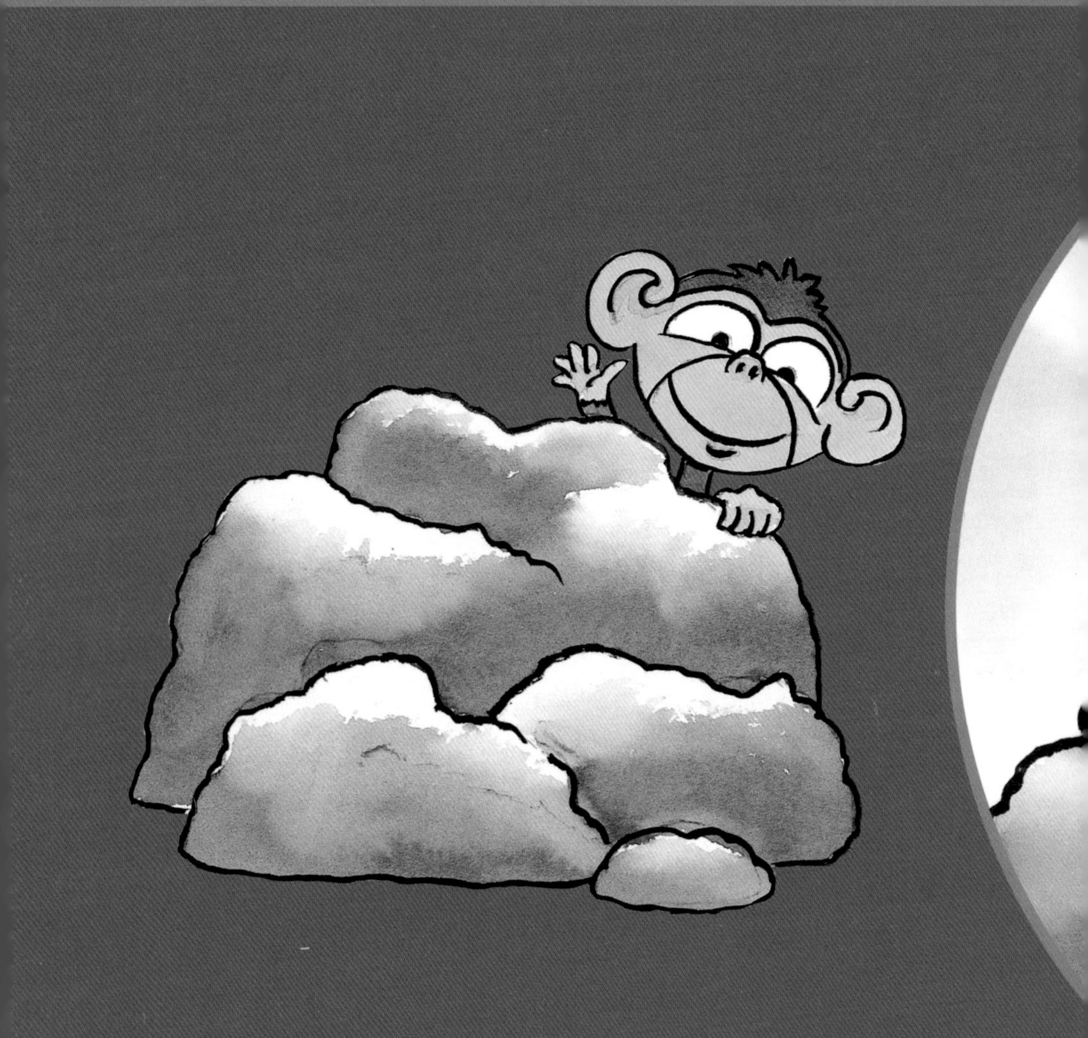

Come to the rock.

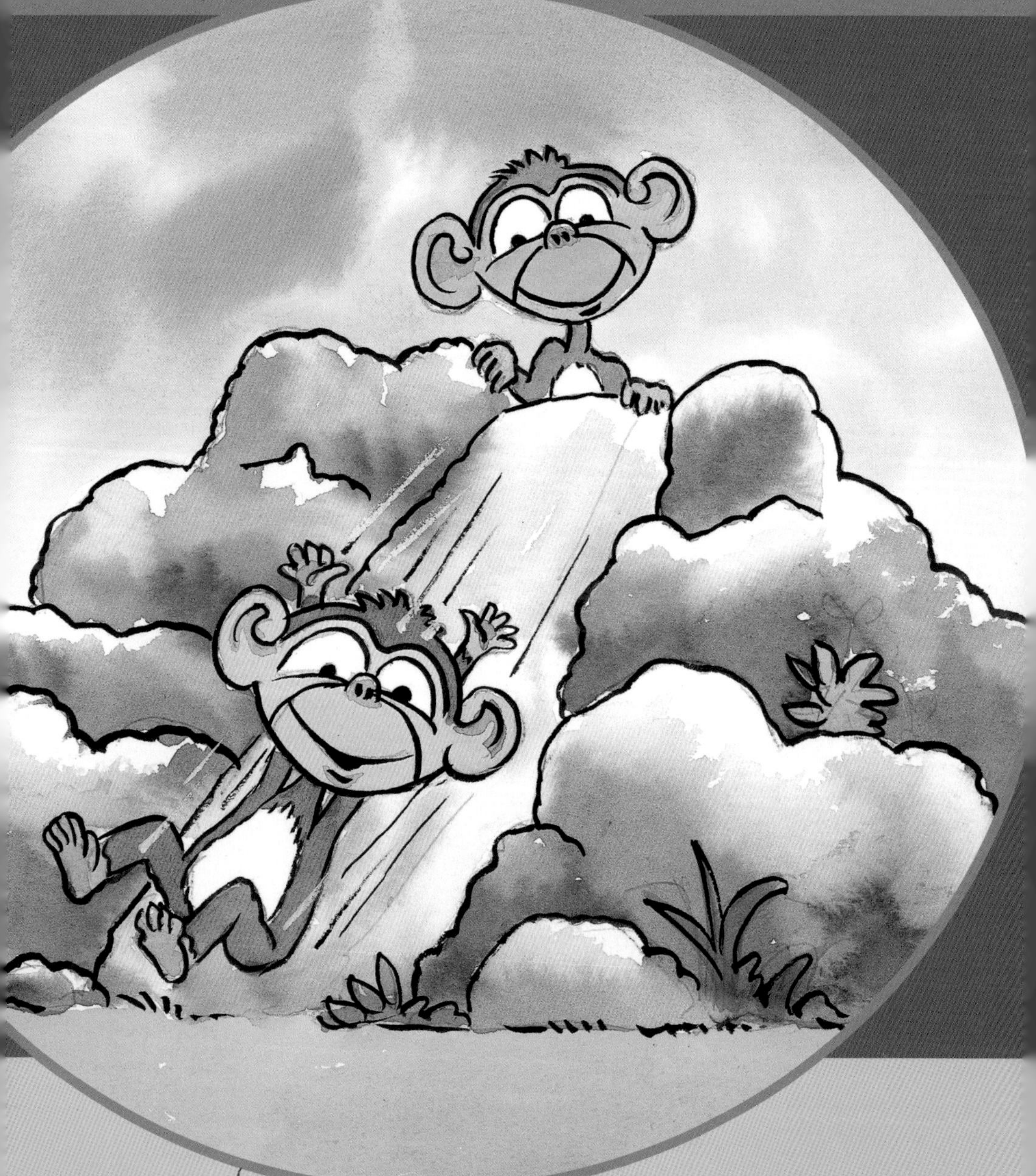

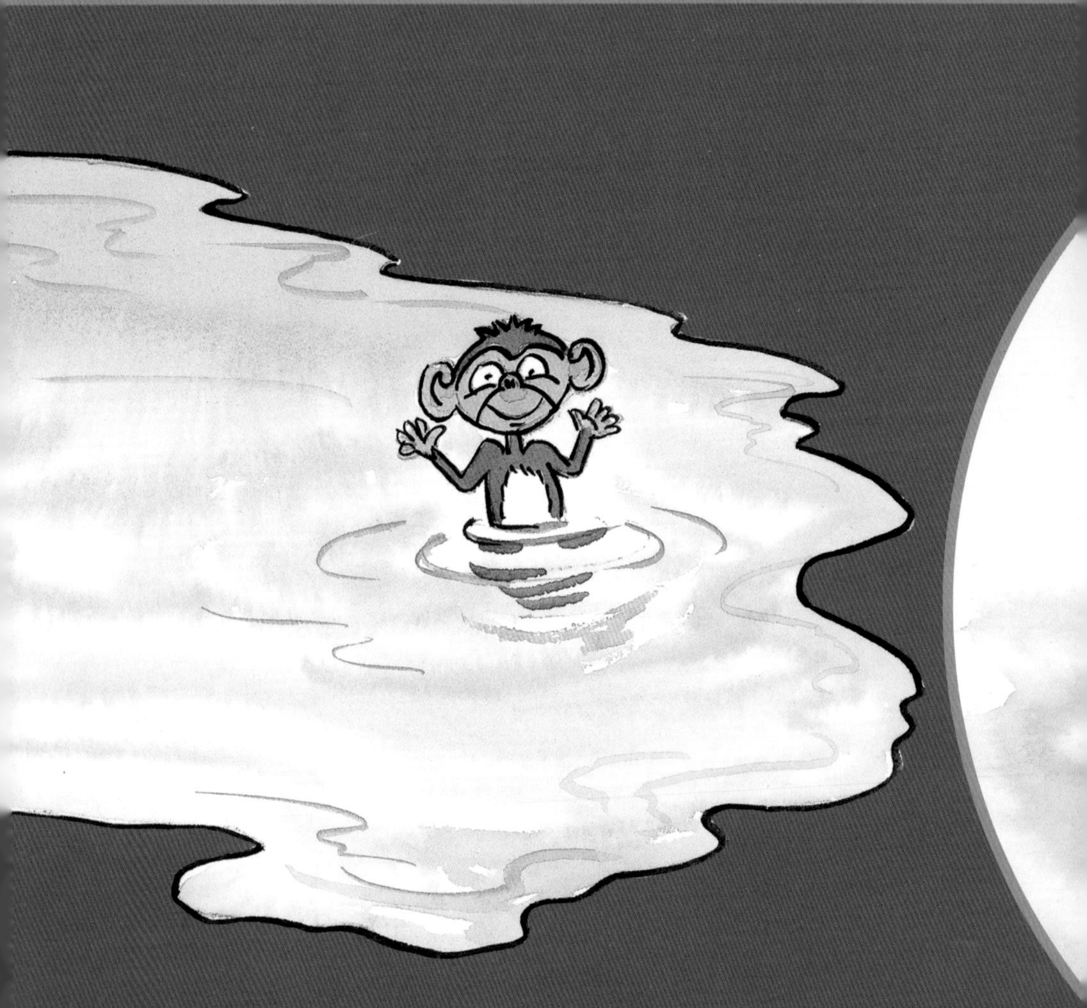

Come to the water.

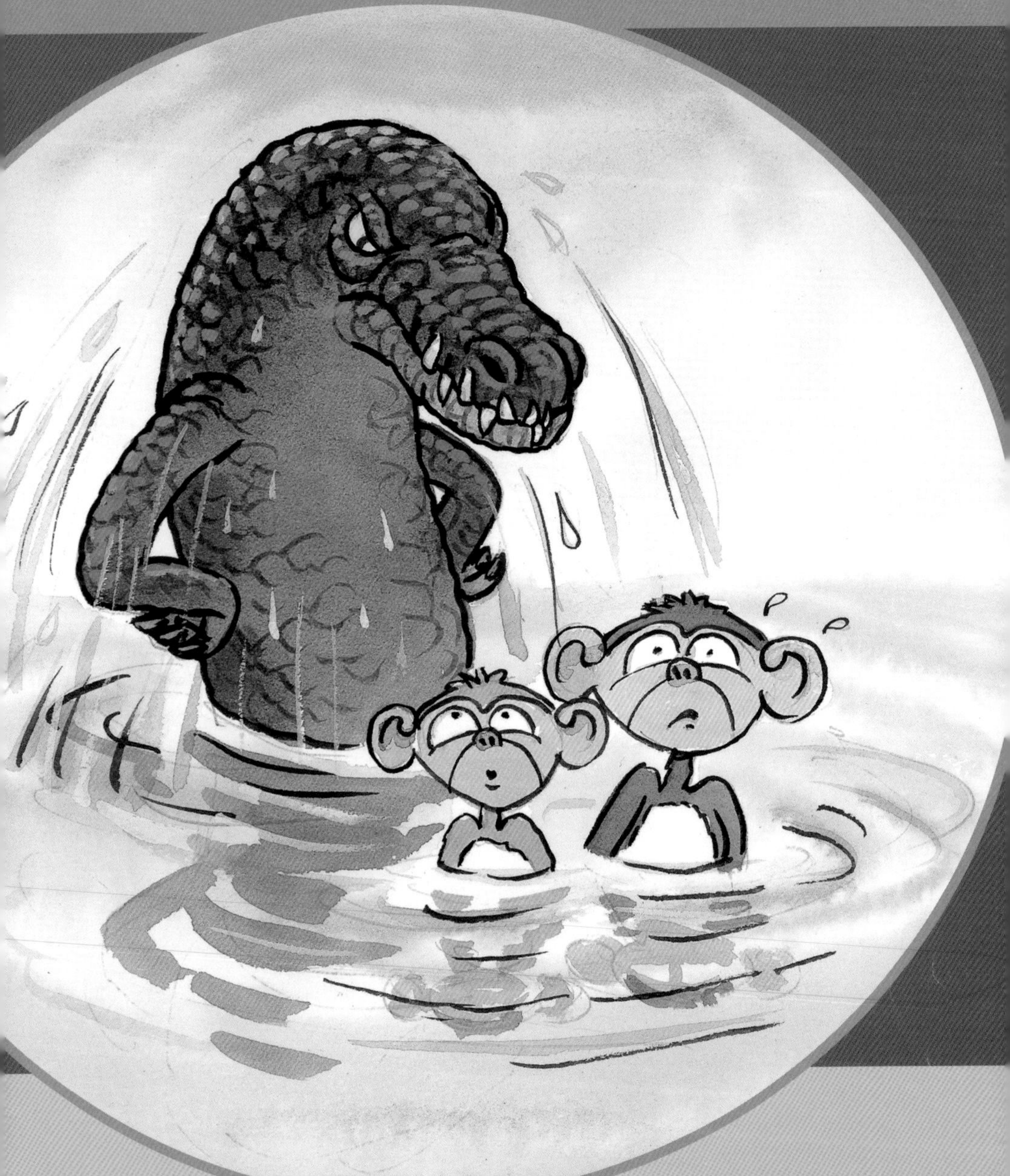

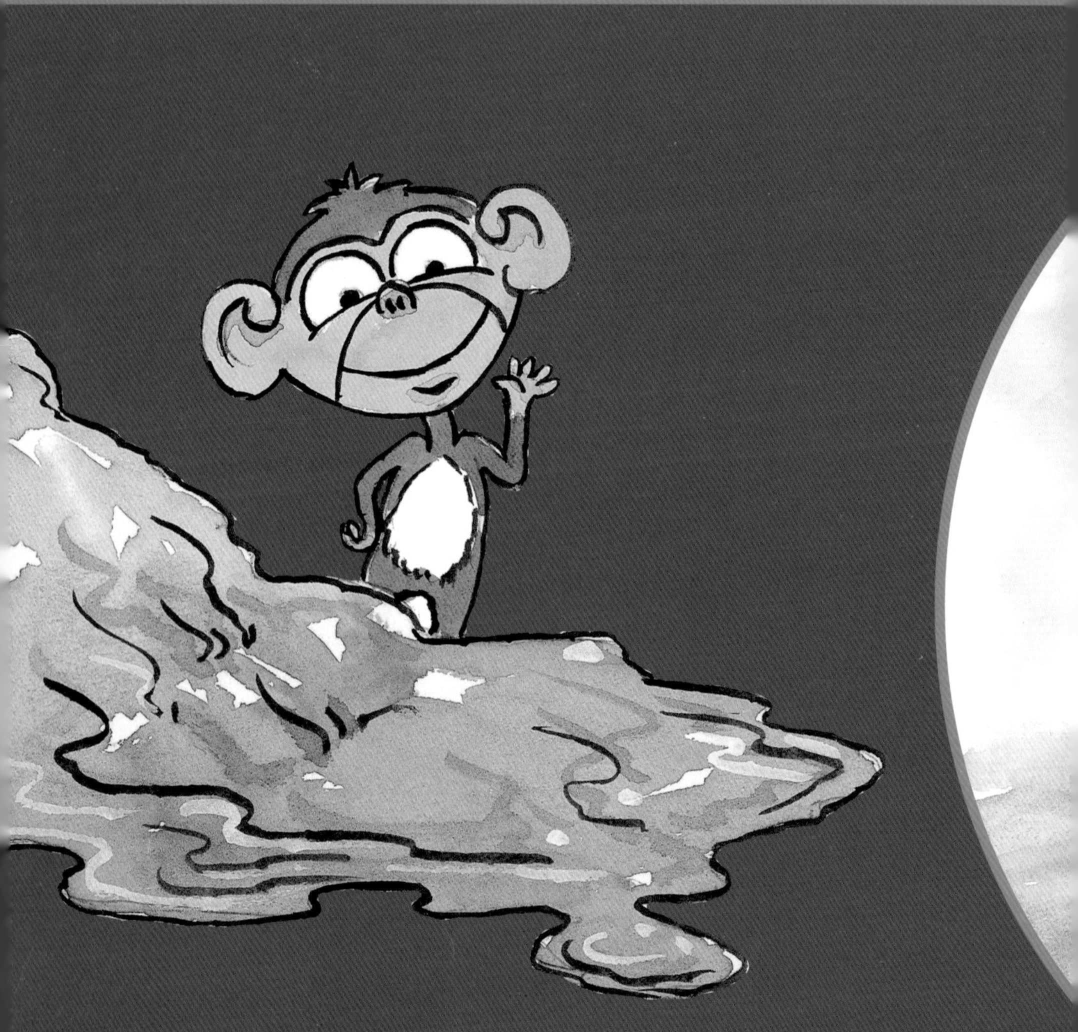

Come to the mud.

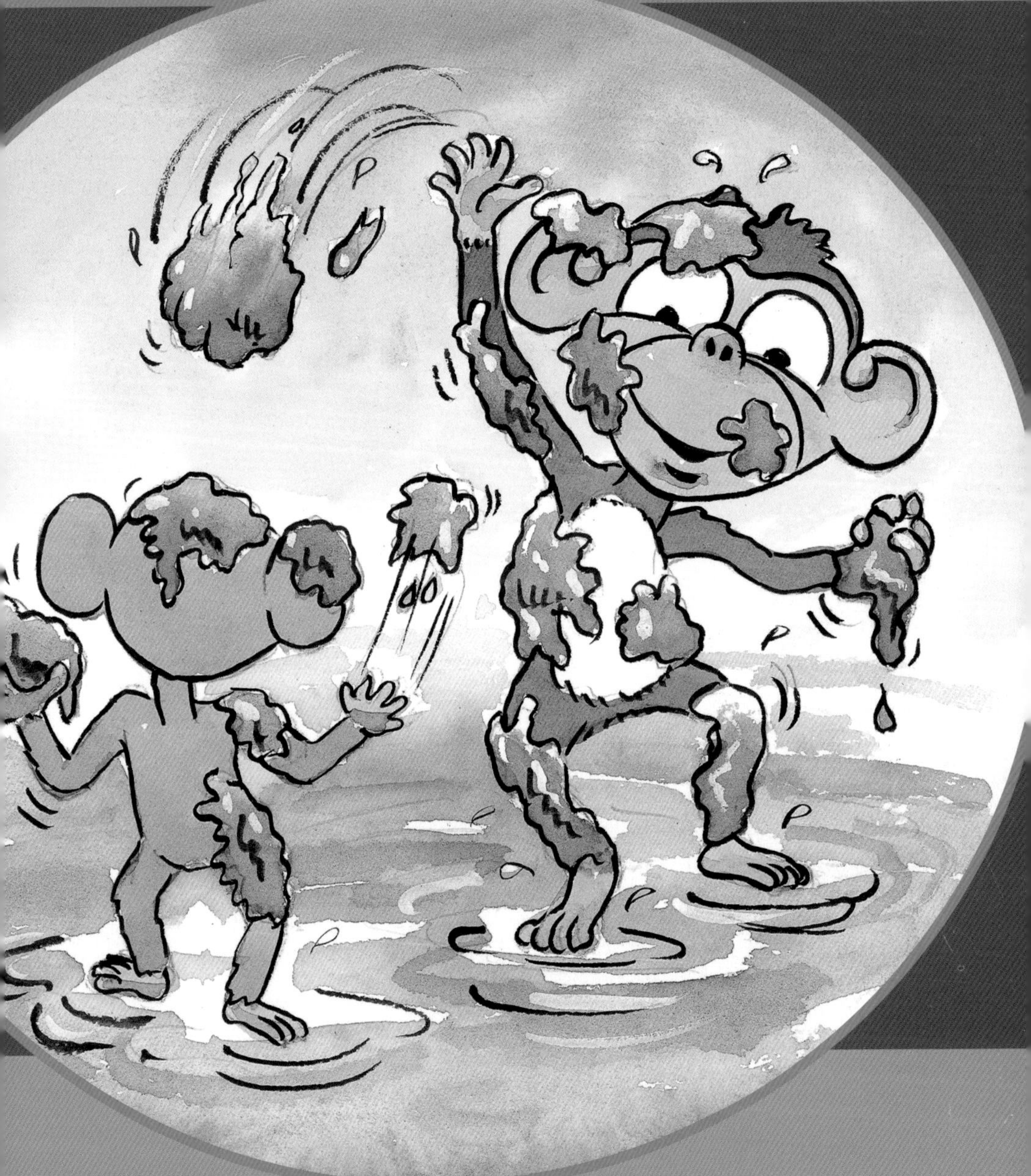

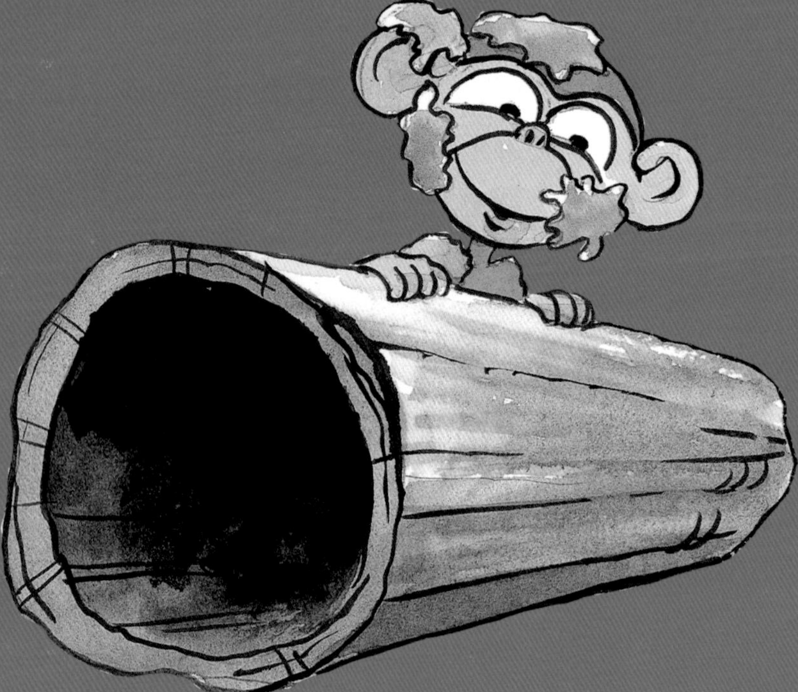

Come to the hole.

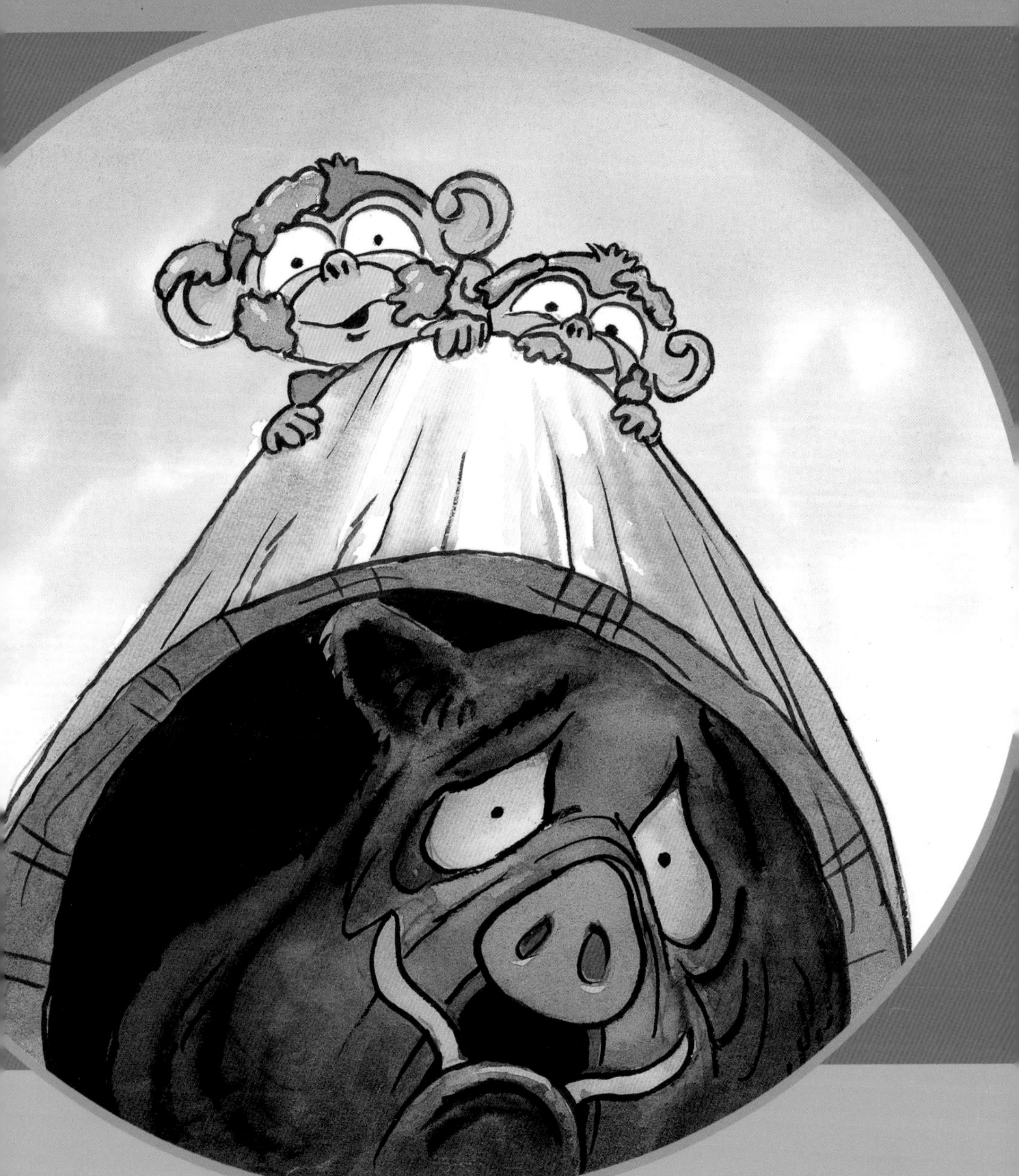

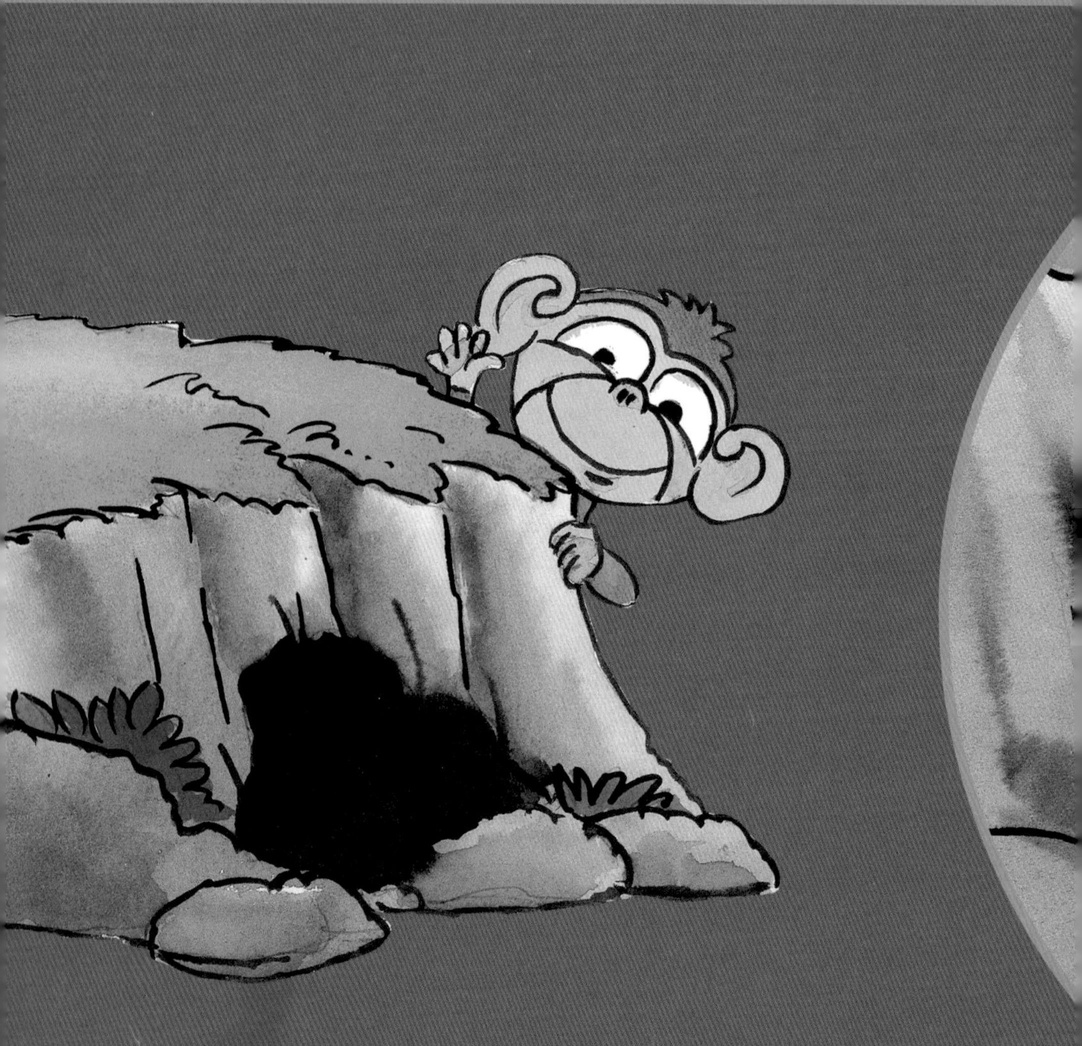

Come to the cave.

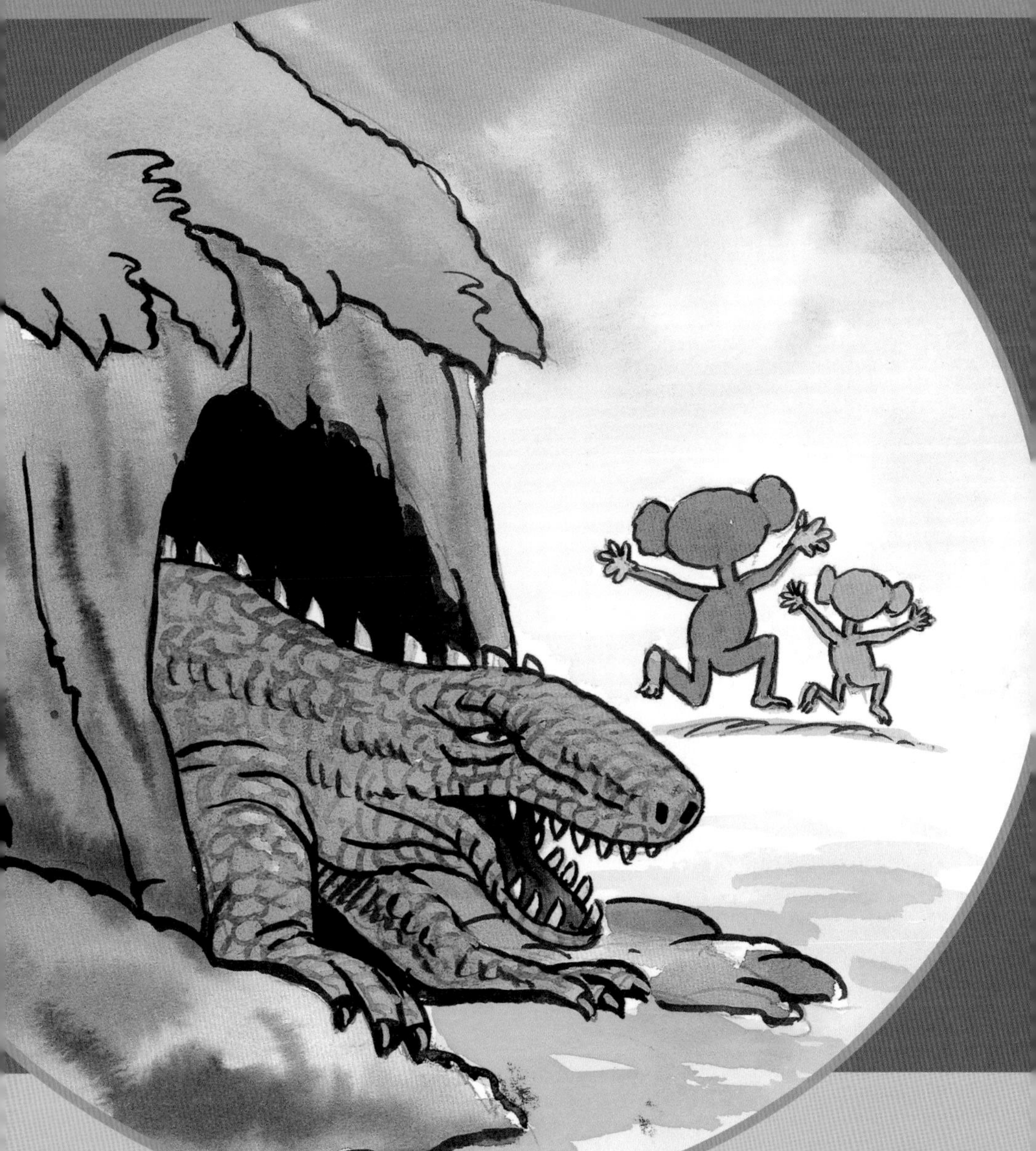

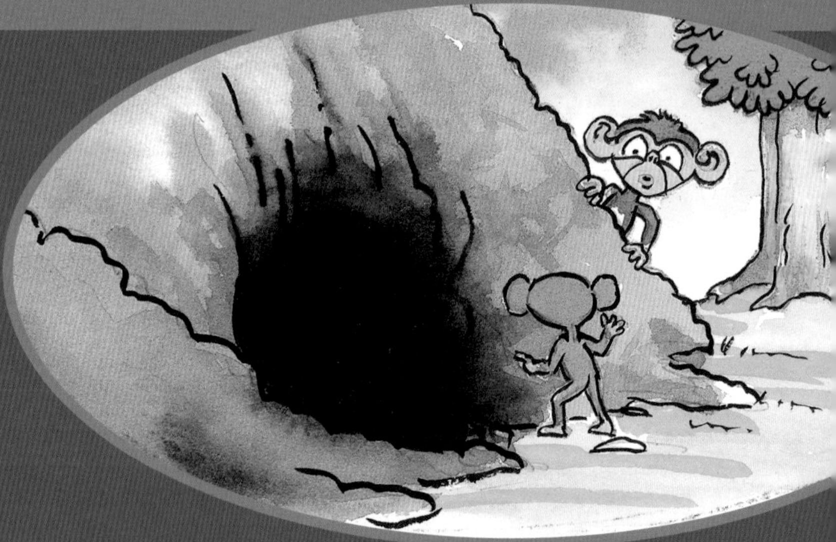

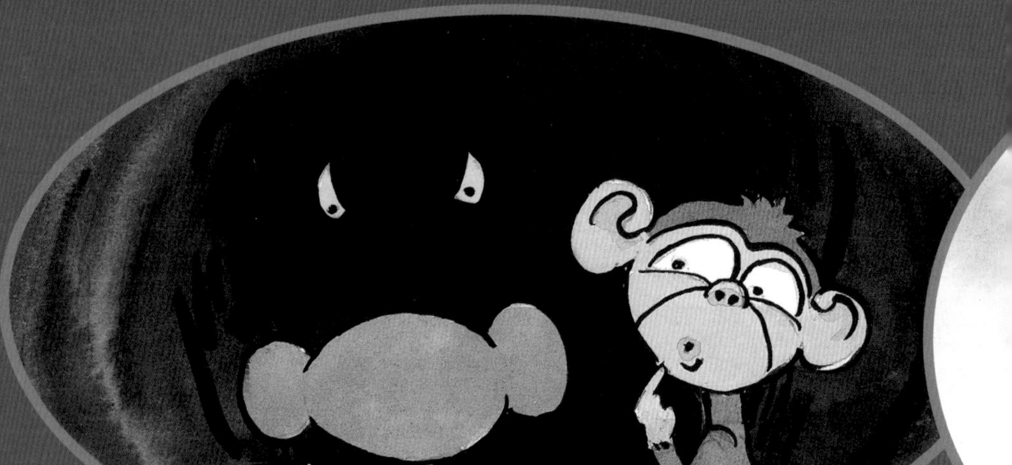

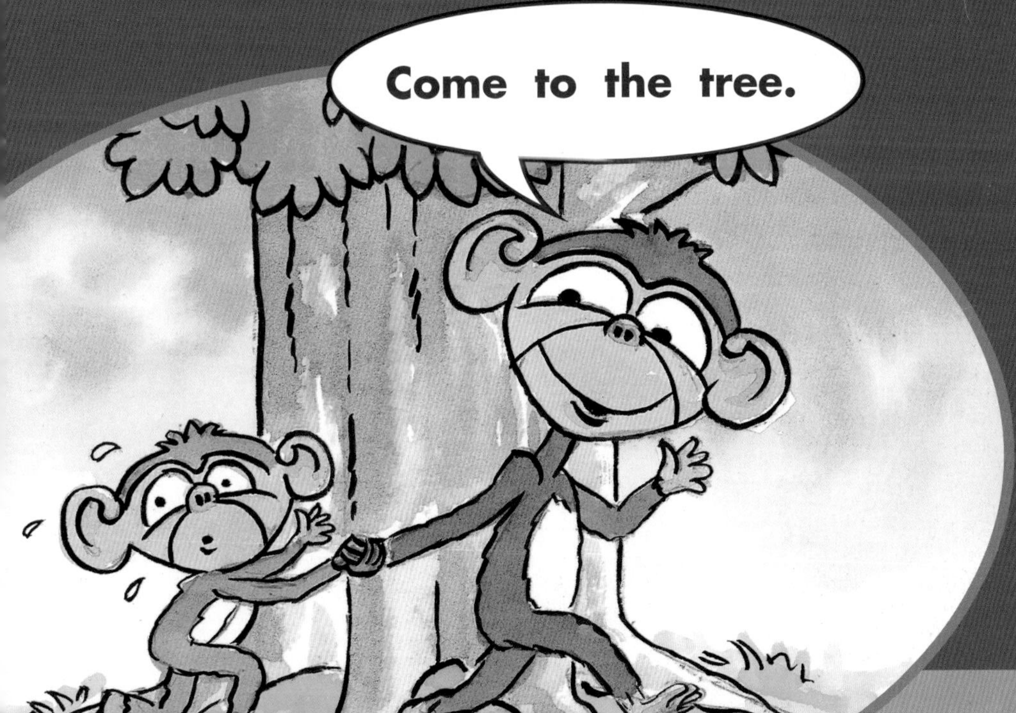
Come to the tree.

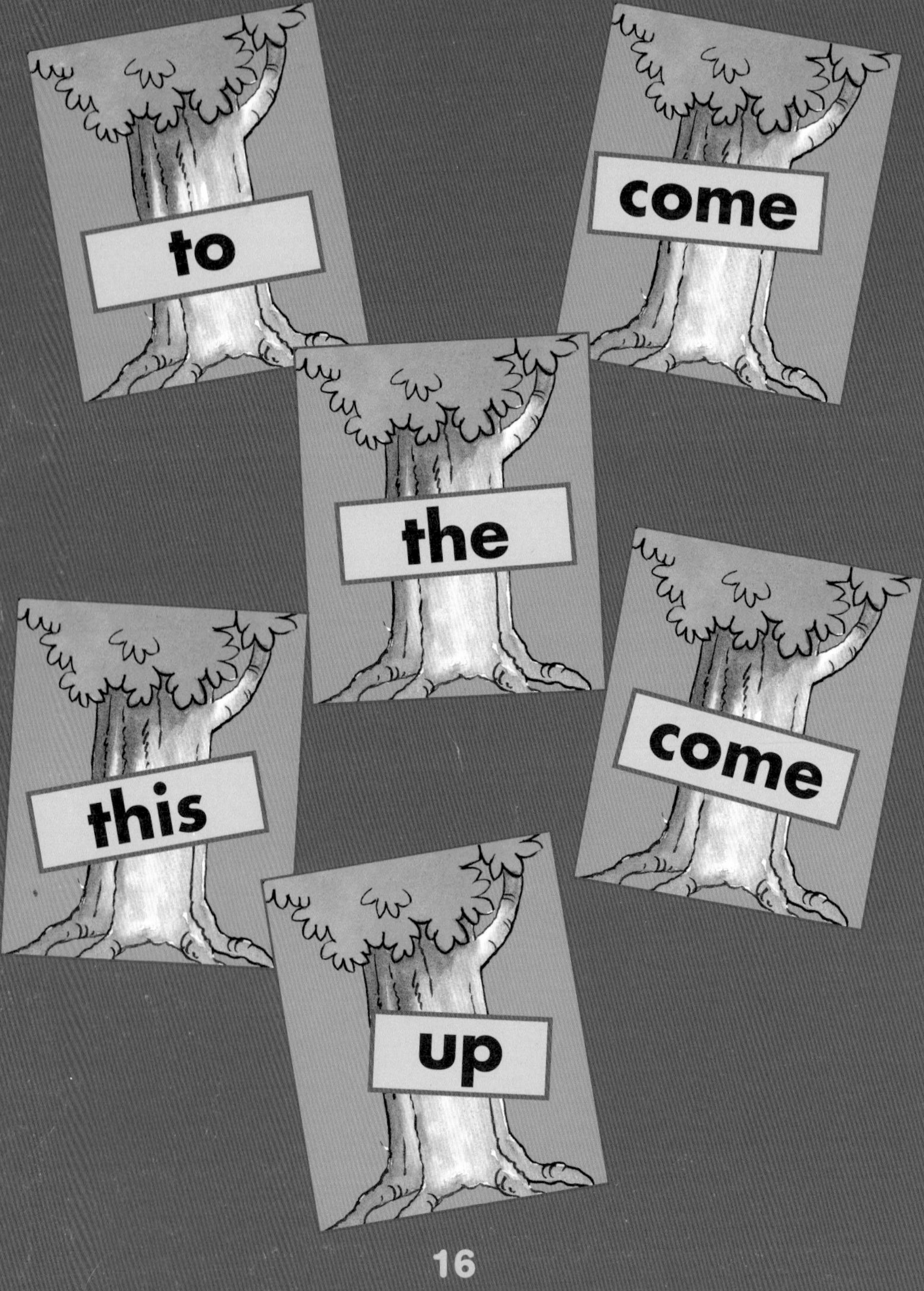
to
come
the
this
come
up